Introduction

In the popular imagination reptiles are not often considered as pets ; yet undeniably this attitude is changing. Reptiles can be kept quite easily : they neither make undue mess nor have to be taken out for walks. And many are beautiful : a Boa Constrictor, an Iguana, or a Rhinoceros Viper can be as attractive as any bird or tropical fish. Although perhaps not as friendly as a dog or cat, an alligator or tortoise can be nearly as lovable ; and with a lot still to be learned about them, the pet keeper is in an ideal position to make fresh discoveries and observations. The adventurous reptile keeper will perhaps want to breed from his stock : there are a number of species that have not yet been reared in captivity.

It is particularly important to have somewhere to house the reptile before it is either bought or caught. This preparation is necessary because of the heat it may need, and also because most reptiles are very talented escapers. The next chapter deals with housing, but it may be a good idea for the reader to consult first the chapters on the various kinds of reptiles : this should ensure the preparation of the right type of vivarium or terrarium.

The vivarium is a specialist cage for various kinds of small creatures needing rather more than just an ordinary box to live in. In the vivarium it is essential to try to create a microcosm of the natural habitat to which the reptile is accustomed.

The requirements for this 'creation', requirements of heat, food, light, and space, will probably influence the ultimate choice of reptile. The pet-owner must be satisfied that he can keep his choice of pet warm and fed, and provide it with enough light and space. A small vivarium for a few lizards, for example, could easily be warmed by a 40 watt light bulb, but a large python or boa would need several 250 watt radiant lights to reach a satisfactory temperature. The lizards may feed happily on earthworms, raw egg, and minced meat, but the python may require several whole chickens or rabbits each week. The contrast is an extreme one, but it does emphasise the importance of thinking carefully about the availability of a regular supply of the right food : a snake may readily accept brown-and-white or nearly black mice, but may appear indifferent to white mice. In virtually all cases the food must be freshly killed ; if the scent and body heat are lacking it seems merely an object rather than food, and may be rejected — even by a starving reptile.

Space is essential for the healthy growth of all reptiles. Some may appear to do well and to feed better with barely enough room

A well-laid-out vivarium

Contents

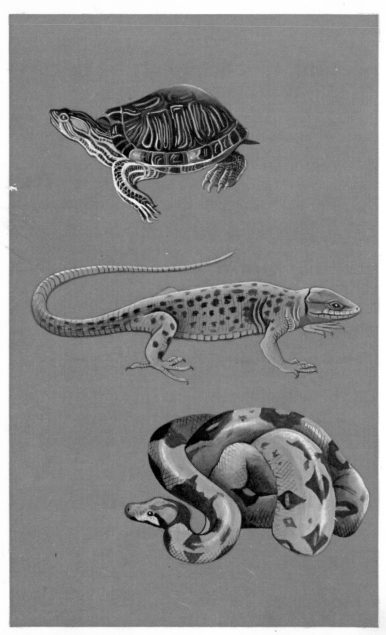

to turn round, but their normal growth rate is restricted. Contrary to the views of some writers, snakes do stretch themselves out, and very lively reptiles like basilisks, monitors, and the racer snakes will injure themselves if artificially restricted.

Another paramount consideration in the choice of a reptile is the availability of the species. Reptile exports are banned from both Australia and New Zealand, and Mississippi alligators are vigorously protected. India, too, has banned the export of nearly all its native fauna. Importing, on the other hand, is not usually restricted, although it is wise to check government regulations before making any arrangements. The beginner would probably be best advised to purchase only those specimens readily available in his own country. Most reputable pet dealers can supply reptiles, although these are generally supplied to order — via specialist dealers — rather than from stock. These specialist dealers will usually send a list of their stock to any potential customer. Some of these lists are very comprehensive, suggesting the diet and living conditions of the reptiles; and most give the creature's Latin names. The Latin name is frequently more useful than simply the common name: the crag lizard, for example, is called *Pseudocordylus subviridis*; the common name merely hints that the lizard is found on crags, but the Latin explains that it is like the cordylus lizard and is green underneath. Colloquially, several species may be called crag or rock lizards, but only one kind can properly be called *Pseudocordylus subviridis*.

The first, or generic, name is always written with an initial capital and will be shared by all the specimens in the group or genus. Hence all the main genus of crocodiles are *C. niloticus, C. cataphractus, C. palustris,* etc. A third word after the specific name will signify a sub-species, so *Pseudemys scripta elegans* indicates that the specimen in question is the Elegant terrapin, not just a Redeared terrapin. The third word is commonly used only by experts, since except in cases where there are many variations, such as terrapins, colubrid water snakes, and skinks, it may only cause confusion. Sometimes the last two words will be the same, indicating that the specimen is the original of which the others with different sub-specific names are slight variations. At first this terminology may be bewildering, but in time the Latin names will roll off the tongue more easily than the more common ones.

Housing your reptile

Home vivaria can be made from a variety of materials, their relative suitability depending upon which species of reptile are to be kept. Vivaria constructed of glass, metal, and wood all have certain advantages and disadvantages, so it is necessary to assess these in the light of the species that have been chosen.

Glass aquarium tanks are frequently used by private herpetologists who have seen them in use in reptile dealer's premises. In fact, there is a tendency among amateurs to look upon such aquaria as the perfect housing solution. This is just not so. The only species that should be kept in aquaria are terrapins, turtles, or crocodilians, and in these cases the vivarium will have to be nearly all water, in fact, an aquarium with land space. The main disadvantage of glass containers is the tremendous heat-loss incurred. This applies also to metal vivaria, though here the fault can be remedied by covering three sides and the base with expanded-polystyrene ceiling tiles.

Condensation is a problem in all uninsulated vivaria as it constitutes a health hazard. Although it can be overcome by increased ventilation this will impair the heat retention of the vivarium still further. Whilst a few reptiles appreciate a moist atmosphere, the vast majority of snakes and lizards (even those which in the natural state bathe quite frequently) require perfectly dry surroundings if they are to thrive. Reptiles kept in too damp an environment soon lose condition and develop small raised blisters on their skins. Since such blisters are difficult to eradicate it is essential that proper humidity be maintained.

The best vivarium is a wooden box, with a hinged lid and a glass front. The floor, sides, and back can either be cut from sheet wood or made from tongued and grooved boards. Plywood and hardboard are not suitable, being easily warped by the heat. The lid should have cut-outs covered with perforated zinc to allow ventilation. Wire netting should never be used in vivarium construction, either as part of a viewing area or for ventilation purposes, since many reptiles will persistently rub against this material in an effort to escape, thus causing permanent damage to the snout. This is especially true of the larger snakes and of monitor lizards. To prevent escapes the lid should be tight fitting with both a catch and a lock.

The interior of a wooden vivarium should have several coats of gloss paint. Modern polyurathene paints are excellent for this; a pastel shade of green or blue is best, white showing the dirt too

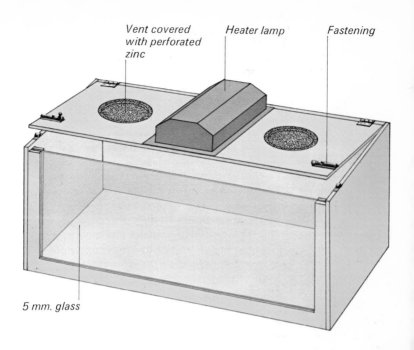

Vent covered with perforated zinc

Heater lamp

Fastening

5 mm. glass

A wooden-box vivarium

easily and reflecting so much light that the specimen will hide from the glare. Unless painted by an expert, scenic backgrounds merely detract from the appearance of a small unit, which will seem lost in a mass of detail. The outside can be either painted or stained to match any surrounding furniture, but this should be done after the internal painting so that nothing is visible or accessible to the specimen.

A lid offers the best method of gaining access to the vivarium, but alternatives include a sliding glass front, a door in the back or side and even the use of a vivarium which lifts off its base. Strong glass is essential in the front, not to prevent escaping but to guard against breakage from outside — a far more likely occurrence. Five milli-metre glass is suitable for all but the largest reptiles, but care must be taken that no large objects such as rocks or plant pots could topple against the glass.

Furnishing the vivarium

The floor covering of the vivarium is highly important to the health of the inmates. Sand should not be used, except for small, desert species, since it clogs up nostrils, irritates the eyes, and contaminates the food. In the case of snakes it can also become lodged under the belly scales, initially causing severe discomfort and, later, infection and swelling.

For burrowing reptiles such as sand boas and horned toads the fine gravel sold by pet shops for use in fish tanks is the perfect answer. It does not clog, and if washed and dried properly before use will not create dust. Remember that a burrowing reptile will deposit its faeces or dung underground, so the gravel should be sifted regularly to remove this. It is advisable to replace the floor covering every few months, or alternatively to boil and dry the used gravel. To ensure that any parasite eggs die before the host reptile is in contact with them, boiled gravel should not be returned to the vivarium for at least a week. For the majority of reptiles, smooth-textured gravel which will not pass through a one-centimetre mesh is suitable. The bigger the reptile the larger the gravel that can be used, although there is little point in using anything that would be stopped by a three-centimetre mesh.

Reptiles which need a slightly damp environment, such as green iguanas and the semi-aquatic mangrove snakes, are best catered for with a layer of moist peat which should be soaked, mixed, and wrung nearly dry before use. Leaves make an effective floor covering and are more retentive of moisture than gravel, though less so than peat.

Rocks of some kind are a necessity in a vivarium, both for aesthetic purposes and to provide cover for the specimens. Some reptiles may be excessively shy and secretive, needing an abundance of hiding places in order to thrive. Sections of cork bark as sold by florists have the advantage of being light and thus incapable of breaking the glass or causing injury to a specimen should it become trapped underneath. Climbing reptiles must be supplied with firm branches, on which they will spend most of their time. Position these with care so that they remain stable when the reptile is clambering over them. There must be no possibility of access to lighting or heating elements, for the natural reaction will be to get close to them, and the result may be a burned snake or lizard.

Fresh water must always be provided and should be changed every day. The requirements of different specimens differ with their habits, but as a general rule the water-container should be

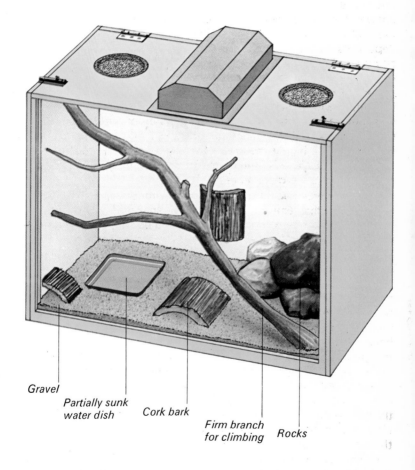

Gravel

Partially sunk
water dish

Cork bark

Firm branch
for climbing

Rocks

Furnishing for most types of vivaria

a flat dish in which the creature can just submerge completely: flower-pot troughs and plastic cat-litter trays are ideal. The siting of the water-dish is important. At best it should be partly sunk into the floor-covering material midway between the side of the vivarium and the space directly under the heater. While reptiles go into water to cool off, they should not be allowed to lose body heat too rapidly, as would happen if some heat from above were not maintaining the temperature of the water. Water is used in the vivarium for aquatic species such as terrapins and small crocodilians. In these cases it is best that the whole vivarium be waterproof and flooded. Gravel should not be provided, just one or two smooth flat rocks under the light or heater for the specimen to bask upon, care being taken that the partly submerged rocks cannot trap it. A wooden platform can be used but it will need to be weighted or wedged to keep it in place. Although such an arrangement is less pleasing aesthetically than other types of vivaria, it is easier to keep clean and odourless.

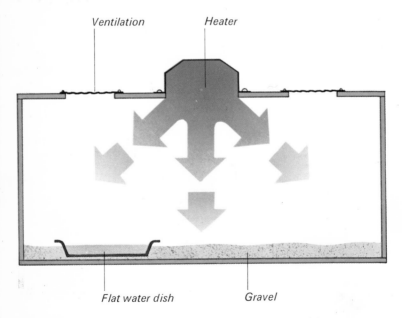

Side elevation of a vivarium showing the correct position of the water dish: this should be partially sunk into the floor covering, midway between the vivarium side and the area directly beneath the heat source.

Heating

Practically all reptiles require a warm and light environment if they are to flourish. Temperature requirements vary, but the majority of reptiles can be kept successfully at between 24°C and 30°C. This is an ambient daytime temperature, and a drop to 18°C is necessary at night to maintain perfect health.

Radiant heat is most suitable for the majority of reptiles and is obtained in the vivarium by using a household lamp or infra-red lamp fixed to the ceiling. In small, home vivaria an ordinary electric light bulb of 100 watts is appropriate, but this should be adapted as necessary to maintain the required temperature in a particular vivarium. The supply to the lamp should be connected to a thermostat to prevent overheating, the most commonly used type of thermostat (made of tubular glass) being sold by most pet shops. One of these placed a little way from the heat source will give the right temperature without any adjustment — a hot spot under the light where the animal can bask, and cooler areas further from the heat source to which it can retire if it becomes overheated. If cool

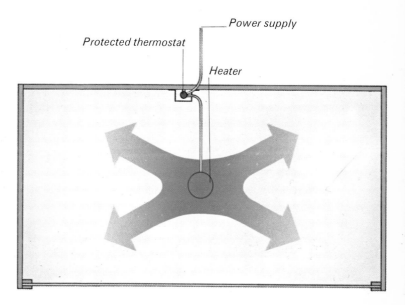

Power supply

Protected thermostat

Heater

Plan of a vivarium showing a pattern of heat radiation that allows both warmer and cooler areas.

places are not provided the specimen may suffer; more pet reptiles die from too much than too little heat.

Underfloor heating has been employed with some success in vivaria, but on the whole this method is unsatisfactory. In its natural habitat the reptile obtains warmth from the sun's rays by basking in them, retiring to shade should they be too strong. Many reptiles will burrow to escape intense heat, so the physiological effect of heating from below is obviously detrimental to their health. Many lizards on show in public vivaria thus suffer from swollen feet and sores on the belly caused by underfloor heating. In large vivaria such heating may be economically necessary; however, if it is the only method available then only certain parts of the floor should be warmed, so that as with the use of radiant heat both hot spots and cool retreats are still available. Naturally, no element used in under-floor heating should be accessible to the reptile, even when it burrows — the use of a sealed container of heat-conducting material will ensure this.

When a radiant heat source is used there should be little need for further lighting, though if appropriate a fluorescent tube of suitable size can be employed. Experiments using ultra-violet light as a sub-stitute for sunlight suggest that, while beneficial if used correctly, it can in excess be very harmful to the reptile. It is used by the authors only in small doses, as a medical aid to sick animals.

Aquarium water heaters, which may be used when keeping aquatic chelonians or crocodilians, should be protected by a cage of perforated zinc or other metal to prevent breakage.

Snakes

Snakes are undoubtedly the most maligned creatures in the animal kingdom, a state of affairs brought about by superstition and ignorance. Without exception they are beautiful, clean creatures, many species adapting themselves readily to captive conditions. Of the 2,700-odd species known, only a mere handful are venomous, and only a relatively small number of these are capable of seriously harming human beings.

It is beyond the scope of this book to tackle all the species suitable for vivarium enthusiasts, but a good cross-section of those usually offered for sale can be introduced. Any closely related species which may be acquired can be cared for along the same lines.

Feeding

All snakes swallow their prey whole, whether it consists of insects, fish, amphibians, mammals, or birds, and this is made possible by the manoeuvrability of the loosely connected jawbones and the elasticity of the skin. Snakes rely mainly on scent to find their prey — the constantly flickering tongue picks up particles from the ground and transfers them to a sense organ, known as Jacobson's organ, situated in the roof of the mouth.

Many arguments have raged over the necessity of feeding live prey to snakes. Whilst it is true that a snake can deal quickly and painlessly with any prey it may want to eat, it must always be remembered that when rodents are used for feeding there is the possibility that the prey may turn on the snake. A snake in this situation, whether it be a powerful constrictor or a venomous species, will often fail to retaliate and may sustain fatal injuries. Nearly all captive snakes, even those coming straight from their natural environment, will accept dead prey and it is much safer for the snake. Should an occasion arise where live food has to be used, both the comfort of the prey and the safety of the snake is assisted by leaving food for the prey in the vivarium as well.

Rodent-eating species are fed on mice, rats, or rabbits, according to species and size. Guinea pigs (cavies) should never be given to reptiles as their exceedingly tough hair and skin can cause severe digestive troubles. The quantity of food given at each meal, usually weekly, obviously depends on the size and species of snake. The smaller, active ones need more food in relation to their size than the larger, more lethargic species — hence a four foot rat snake would

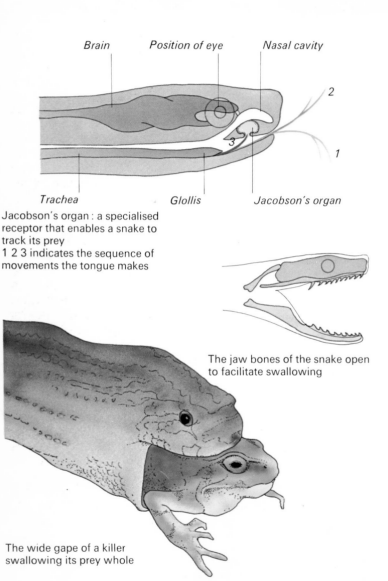

Brain   Position of eye   Nasal cavity

2

3

1

Trachea   Glollis   Jacobson's organ

Jacobson's organ : a specialised receptor that enables a snake to track its prey
1 2 3 indicates the sequence of movements the tongue makes

The jaw bones of the snake open to facilitate swallowing

The wide gape of a killer swallowing its prey whole

need about three or four adult mice a week, whereas one rabbit would probably keep a twelve foot python happy for a fortnight. Snakes should not be allowed to gorge themselves too heavily, since, especially in captivity, they have a tendency to put on excess body fat at an alarming rate. A healthy snake should have a well-rounded body without being fat; it is best always to keep your specimen a little hungry so as to maintain its interest in food.

Hunger strike is a problem frequently encountered with captive snakes. Usually it occurs in recently imported animals, and every effort should be made to provide such snakes with as wide a variety of food as possible: a snake coming straight from the wild may not recognise a white mouse as food, yet it may well take to a brown one or perhaps a small gerbil. Raising the temperature in the vivarium may encourage the snake to take food. If this is unsuccessful, turning off all the lights and leaving the specimen in total darkness may help. It is amazing how easily a staring human may put a shy reptile off its meal, so the owner should curb his enthusiasm for a while and leave the snake alone after providing its food. Forced feeding is sometimes advocated in cases of hunger strike, but is likely to encourage rather than postpone the animal's death. A snake is a very delicate creature, and attempts to stuff food down its throat — which will probably be regurgitated later — are far from beneficial. If kept in suitable surroundings and offered the correct food the snake should eat sooner or later; if it does not it is possible that the creature is sick or physically damaged, perhaps as a result of transportation. Of course, it is best that the prospective owner see an individual snake feed before he purchases it.

Sometimes a well-established vivarium snake will go on a hunger strike for several weeks or months, and then begin to feed again. This is often the habit of snakes that would, in their native countries, either hibernate or be affected by drought, and provided the snake has been looked after, such a long fast can do the reptile no harm — in some cases it may even be beneficial.

Most snakes which in their natural state feed on birds can easily be catered for with day-old chicks. Often these can be readily and quickly obtained from commercial hatcheries when the undersized ones are destroyed after sorting.

Species such as garter and water snakes, which habitually feed off live fish, can be coaxed into taking fresh sprats or strips of flesh from larger fish. Initially they must be tempted with live minnows or goldfish, but most will soon adapt to more available food.

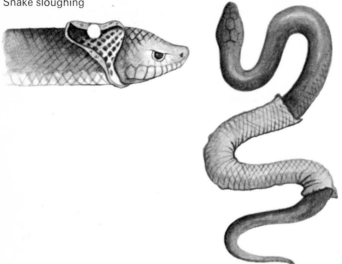

Sloughing

Due to growth or wear and tear, snakes frequently cast off their outer skin in the process called *sloughing* (pronounced *sluffing*). This happens far more frequently than is generally realised: a young, healthy snake perhaps sloughing every four weeks. When about to slough, a snake secretes, between the newly-formed and the old skin, a layer of liquid which can be seen through the transparent eye scales. During this period the animal keeps well hidden, usually refusing all food. The milky appearance soon disappears and the snake then rubs its snout against rough, firm objects in order to break the skin: rocks and branches should thus be provided in the vivarium for this purpose. Eventually the skin splits and by constant rubbing of its body, the snake escapes from the old skin and usually leaves it in one piece, inside-out.

Sometimes vivarium snakes require help in sloughing. If specimens in this condition can be confined in a bath of water at a temperature of 24°C for several hours, this will soften the skin and enable it to be gently removed. It is often beneficial for the snake to be sprayed with water, occasionally, during the slough, but if the drinking facilities allow the reptile to immerse itself in the water no problems need occur.

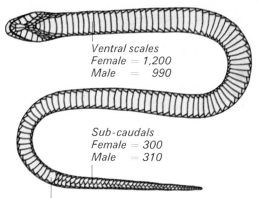

Ventral scales
Female = 1,200
Male = 990

Sub-caudals
Female = 300
Male = 310

Anal plate

Underside of snake

The main difference between male and female snakes is that the female has more ventral scales, and therefore a longer body than the male, but the female has less sub-caudals, making its tail slightly shorter than that of the male.

Breeding

Unfortunately, snakes, like all reptiles, do not breed easily in captivity. This is no reason why herpetologists should keep single specimens, however, since several species have bred in the care of private collectors, and doubtless if people took the trouble to purchase a sexed pair initially, the number could be increased.

Live-bearing, or viviparous, species, such as boas, garter and water snakes, seem to breed more freely in captivity than the egg-laying, or oviparous ones. Should the herpetologist have the good luck to succeed, he stands a good chance of rearing the youngsters. Baby snakes usually begin feeding after their first slough, which takes place a few days after birth. The young of water and garter snakes, perhaps the most easily bred of all reptiles in captivity, can usually be started on small fish, tadpoles, and earthworms, while those of the larger species, including the egg-layers, begin on very small mice, either hairless or very newly-furred. Care should be taken to ensure that the most forward of the brood does not monopolise the food supply; it is therefore wise to separate the heavy feeders from the weak. Young snakes should always be given small food, even when they might manage larger, for they tend to gorge themselves, with burst guts as a result.

19

Egg-laying species are more difficult to rear due to the need for the perfect medium in which to hatch the eggs. Fine sand and leaf mould are best in this respect, although success has been achieved with foam-rubber, newspaper, and even by leaving the eggs suspended in a plastic bag. Whatever medium is used the eggs must be handled as little as possible, although regular checks should be made, and damaged or obviously infertile eggs removed. While a measure of humidity should be maintained, the hatching medium should never become soggy — a constant temperature of about 29°C is needed for the hatching, which takes from five to ten weeks according to the species. Upon hatching, the young can be cared for in the same way as those of viviparous snakes. The snake-breeders main problem is that of sexing his pets. Occasionally the double-structured penis of the male is visible during excretion, but one cannot always wait for this to take place. Generally the female is of a heavier build than the male, and her tail is much shorter and less tapered; the male has a long, slender tail, hard to discern without close examination.

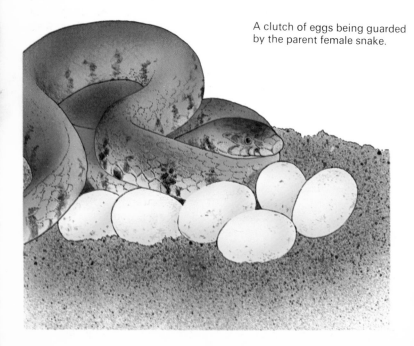

A clutch of eggs being guarded by the parent female snake.

Species suitable for vivaria

Boas and pythons — Boidae
Despite their larger size, the boas and pythons have always been popular with vivarium enthusiasts. Their impressive build, beautiful colours, and usually docile temperament are well known, and most species are equally excellent feeders in captivity. The differences between boas and pythons are few — the former give birth to live young and are found in the New World, while the latter lay eggs and inhabit the Old World. Exceptions to these rules are rare. All snakes in this group kill their prey — usually mammals and birds — by constriction, and not (despite popular belief) by crushing. They coil around their victims and apply great pressure to the neck and rib areas, causing death by suffocation.

The larger pythons actually incubate their eggs. Like all reptiles they are cold-blooded and so unable to alter their body temperature from that of the immediate environment, but having laid the eggs the female python coils around them and manages to raise the temperature of the clutch by a few degrees. The large boas and pythons are usually sold when very young, often not long after birth. They are usually simple to rear, growing very rapidly indeed and often trebling their length during the first year of captivity.

The Boa Constrictor (*Constrictor constrictor*) is perhaps best known among the giant snakes. Inhabiting a wide area of South and Central America, it is often kept by the natives to rid their homes of vermin. The longest recorded length is about eighteen feet, though a twelve footer would be regarded as large. Normally a vivarium boa will be six to eight feet: the snake thrives very well in captivity and has often been bred.

The Rainbow Boa (*Epicrates cenchris*) is far smaller than the Boa Constrictor, rarely exceeding six feet in length. It is a shy, docile snake which rarely bites and, while looking rather dull in a poorly-lit environment, it has a beautiful irridescent sheen on its scales when seen in good light. Largest of all the boas, indeed the world's largest snake, is the South American Anaconda (*Eunectes murinus*). It grows to nearly thirty feet and has an exceedingly heavy girth in proportion to its length. The green colour with large, black spots gives it wonderful camouflage in the murky shallows of forest streams, where it normally resides. In captivity it is prone to irritability and may bite. It must be supplied with a fair-sized pool, where it will probably prefer to take its food. Chicks are the favourite diet of the younger specimens, but rodents are also enjoyed.

South American Boa Constrictor *Constrictor constrictor*

Rainbow Constrictor *Epicrates cenchris*

23

Much smaller are the Sand Boas (genus *Eryx*), from Asia and Africa. The two most commonly imported are the Red and Rough tailed (*E. johni* and *E. conicus*) from South-Eastern Asia. These take fairly well to life in the vivarium, feeding on mice and small birds, but they are prone to go on long hunger strikes and, by way of their burrowing habits, usually hide themselves amid the floor-covering.

Probably the most popular among pythons is the Asian or Indian Rock Python (*Python molurus*), also found throughout South-East Asia. This has two distinct phases, the light phase, which is the stockier sub-species and coloured with pink markings on a cream background, and the more common dark phase, which has dark brown markings with small parts showing yellow. Normally very tractable in captivity, though not without exception, it grows rapidly, if not often beyond half its maximum length of twenty feet. Very closely related and similar in size and temperament, the African Rock Python (*Python sebae*) can be found throughout Africa south of the Sahara. Like the Asian Python, it flourishes in captivity, often growing to an embarassing size.

One of the smallest of the pythons is the West African Royal or Ball Python (*Python regius*). It earns its latter, common, name by its habit or rolling into a tight ball when alarmed, with its head buried deep in its coils for protection. Though its size is ideal from the point of view of the snake-keeper, rarely exceeding five feet, it can be very difficult to establish when imported since it frequently refuses to feed. However, most specimens will accept small gerbils and can, with care and patience, be converted to a more economical diet of mice.

The largest of the pythons is the reticulated species Regal Python (*Python reticulatus*) which has been known to attain a record length of thirty-three feet. Nevertheless, it is a slightly-built reptile ; a fifteen foot specimen coiled up appears little larger than an eight foot boa or anaconda. It is found throughout South-East Asia and frequently imported, yet most specimens are nervous and irritable, biting savagely when handled. Docile specimens are sometimes to be found, however, and because of their considerable size and beautiful colouration they must be one of the most spectacular of all pet snakes.

Reticulated Python Regal Python (USA) *Python reticulatus*

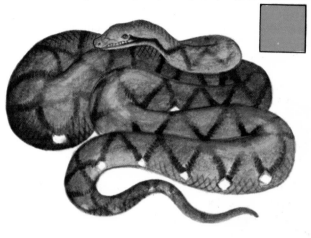

Rock Python *Python molurus*

Colubrids — colubridae

The colubrids are by far the largest group of snakes. Found in a great diversity of forms almost everywhere in the world, they live in a variety of habitats. Many are kept in vivaria — it will be possible to mention only a few.

Watersnakes (genus *Natrix*). American members of this genus, such as the Broad-banded and Red-bellied species, are among the easiest kept of all snakes. Being hardy, they very frequently mate and produce young in captivity, and readily adapt to a diet of strips of raw fish or even raw meat. They grow to a length of four feet. Unfortunately, they sometimes bite savagely and also have the delightful habit of discharging evil-smelling liquid from their anal gland when handled. Although they are normally found near water, a bone-dry vivarium is essential to their well-being. It should contain a large bowl of water, which will be used both for drinking and bathing. Several species of this genus are found in Europe. Similar to their American counterparts, although rarely vicious, they do not commonly thrive so well in captivity. The Diced Watersnake (*Natrix tesselata*) is generally easily fed, preferring live fish — a taste shared by the Common Grass Snake (*Natrix natrix*), the best-known British snake, (or Water Snake [USA]) despite its preference for amphibia such as frogs and newts.

Garter Snakes (genus *Thamnophis*). These are the most familiar of North American reptiles, being found all over the country in a wide range of habitats. The Common Garter Snake (*Thamnophis sirtalis*) is most frequently found in captivity. Only rarely exceeding two feet, it is shy and docile and likes to eat fish and earthworms. Captive births occur often, broods containing over sixty not being unknown.

Rat Snakes (genus *Elaphe*). These medium-sized, fast-moving snakes inhabit the Americas, Europe, Asia, and Africa. All may be termed 'semi-constrictors'; lacking the flexibility of the boas and pythons they often kill their prey rather clumsily, and some species tend to be particularly haphazard. As the name suggests, most species live on rodents, but a bird makes a welcome change and eggs are often consumed. Oviparous rat snakes are fairly active reptiles, requiring a large vivarium equipped with stout branches on which they will enjoy climbing. The most sought-after of the American species is the Corn Snake (*Elaphe guttata*), a handsome red-brown creature averaging three to six feet. Like others of its genus it is happy at a moderate temperature around 24 °C and feeds successfully on mice.

The Black Rat Snake (*E. obsoleta*) is far larger, growing at times to eight feet. Adult specimens are sooty black, while juveniles are light grey with dark markings. Largest of the European species is the Four Line Snake (*Elaphe quatuorlineata*), so named from the stripes down the length of its body, which is similar but not identical to the Yellow Rat Snake (*Elaphe quadrivittata*) of the

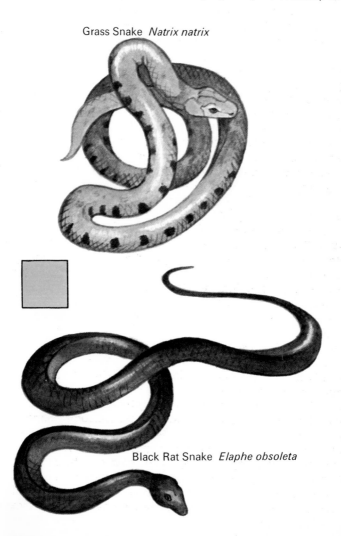

Grass Snake *Natrix natrix*

Black Rat Snake *Elaphe obsoleta*

U.S.A. Several closely allied snakes from Asia are frequently imported by vivarium keepers. The Indian Rat Snake (*Ptyas mucosus*) is perhaps the world's longest colubrid, a plain olive-coloured creature usually tolerant of captivity but at the same time highly-strung and a vicious biter. Snakes of the genus *Spalerosophis*, from North Africa, Asia Minor, and Pakistan are similar in temperament. These, notably the Royal or Diadem Rat Snake, are particularly exquisite in appearance and, if kept warm and dry, live for a long time in a vivarium.

King Snakes (genus *Lampropeltis*). Another group of colubrids from North America, these are medium-sized, powerful reptiles relying on constriction to despatch the small mammals normally comprising their prey. They sometimes attack and eat other snakes, even venomous ones, from whose poison they seem to be imune.

King Snake *Lampropeltis*

For this reason they should not be included in mixed collections and only specimens of similar size should be kept together in case cannibalism should occur. King Snakes are, however, particularly gentle towards humans, and are hardy vivarium inmates.

Mole Snakes (*Pseudaspis cana*). This snake, the sole member of its genus, comes from South Africa and is that country's equivalent of the King Snake. It feeds on other snakes and rodents, especially the burrowing mole-rats from which it derives its name. The shovel-shaped nose is adapted to burrowing, and like the sand boas it commonly spends its time buried under the ground. The normal colouring is greyish-brown with a pink or orange belly, but a rarer, jet-black variety is occasionally imported. In captivity it requires a high temperature, enough floor space to permit burrowing and a few branches on which to climb. It bears live young.

Mole Snake *Pseudaspis cana*

Venomous snakes

Venomous snakes fall into three main groups. Firstly, the *Boiginae,* the rear-fanged Colubrids. These have large teeth at the rear of the upper jaw, which are grooved to allow venom manufactured in the venom gland to trickle down. Generally, these snakes are harmless to man, since the strength of their poison is sufficient only to kill their prey. In fact, it would be difficult for a rear-fanged snake to embed its teeth in a human as they are positioned so far back in the mouth. However, two particular species, the Boomslang (*Dispholidus typus*) and the Bird Snake, or Kirtlands Tree Snake (*Thelotornis Kirtlandi*), both African, have unusually toxic venoms and have frequently been known to cause human deaths. Little is known about the venomous properties of the rear-fanged snakes, and large specimens must be treated with respect.

The second group comprises the *Elapidae,* the cobras, mambas, kraits, and tiger snakes. The *Hydraphiidae,* or sea snakes, are sometimes classed within this group. These have short, ridged fangs at the front of the upper jaw. Venom flows through a channel in each fang and is usually of the neurotoxic type, causing paralysis, especially of the heart and chest muscles.

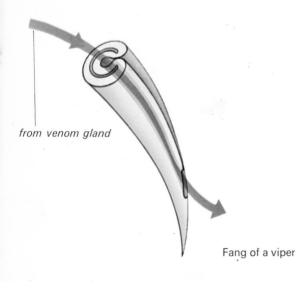

from venom gland

Fang of a viper

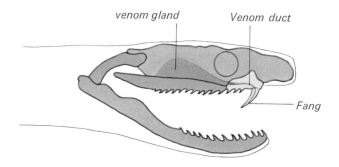

Front fanged Elapidae and Hydraphiidae

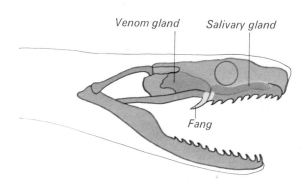

Rear fanged
Mangrove Snake Boiga dendrophila

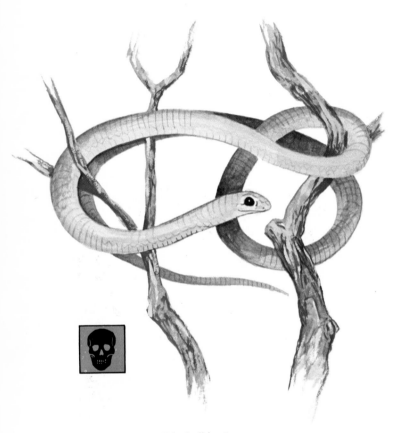

Boomslang *Dispholidus typus*

Tiger Snake – Among the world's most deadly snakes. *Notechis scutatus*

Dangerous front-fanged species should never be kept by amateur herpetologists, unless they are greatly experienced in dealing with a wide variety of snakes. Anyone working with dangerous venomous snakes should have immediate access to supplies of the appropriate serum: almost every year the national press contains reports of individuals who have been bitten by dangerous snakes, or worse still have allowed them to escape. Usually no serum is available and the assistance of the nearest major zoo is invoked. Such incidents bring only discredit to other reptile-keepers, particularly those who keep venomous snakes.

The third group is the *Viperidae*, or vipers, including the *Crotalidae*

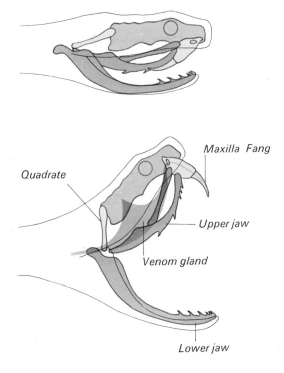

The jaw-bones of a viper are joined to its skull by two hinges of bone (yellow)

or pit vipers. Many well-known venomous snakes are in this category — Russell's Viper, the Rhinoceros Viper, and Gaboon Viper; the European Adder, the Puff Adder, the Rattlesnake, Fer-de-lance, and Bushmaster. These snakes possess the most sophisticated venom apparatus of all the groups, with large fangs situated well to the front of the mouth which fold flat along the jaw when the mouth is shut. When a viper strikes the mouth is opened extremely wide, the fangs swing down and are swiftly embedded in the prey with a stabbing motion. Haemotoxic poison is employed by this group — as the name suggests, the venom destroys blood corpuscles, causes internal bleeding, and serious tissue damage.

Russell's Viper *Vipera russelli*

Bushmaster *Lachesis muta*

Venomous snakes for the vivarium

Several rear-fanged species are frequently offered for sale and these often make suitable vivarium inmates, but one must always bear in mind that they are potentially more dangerous than non-venomous snakes. Care must be taken in handling them, especially the genus *Boidae* — for example, the Mangrove Snake and the large Sand Snakes (*Psamnophis*).

The Flying Snake (*Chrysopelea ornata*) is unusual in having the ability to flatten its body by stretching its ribs; in this way it can glide considerable distances between branches high up in the trees where it normally lives. Despite being somewhat delicate, and so

Flying Snake *Chrysopelea ornata*

susceptible to changes in temperature, it can be kept quite readily and, while preferring its natural diet of lizards, will accept young mice.

The Long-nosed Tree Snake (*Dryophis nasutus*), an incredibly thin, bright-green snake, is frequently offered for sale quite cheaply. However, it is hardly suitable for the vivarium, eating little else but small lizards (of which, for its size, it requires a surprising number). Occasionally one will eat mice, usually babies without fur, but most refuse to and die slowly from starvation. If the reader is offered one he should decline it unless he can be shown the snake eating easily obtainable food.

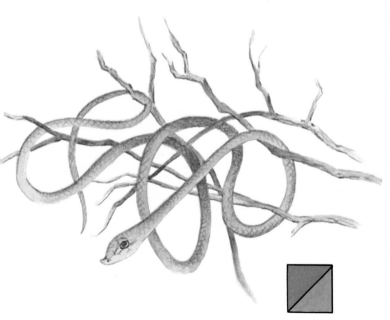

Long-nosed Tree Snake *Dryophis nasutus*

Asian Mangrove Snake *Boiga dendrophila*

Much more suitable for the vivaria are the Sand Snakes (*Psamna-phis*) from Africa and parts of Asia. Usually seen in captivity is the Hissing Sand Snake, or African Beauty (*P. sibilans*). This attractive animal is coloured dark olive, and has large eyes and a particularly alert nature. In a large vivarium, it thrives well and feeds on small rodents. Its maximum length is about four and a half feet.

One of the most beautiful of all snakes is the Asian Mangrove Snake (*Boiga dendrophila*). Growing to over six feet, it is a lustrous black with vivid-yellow vertical bands down the length of its body. This reptile normally lives in the trees of mangrove swamps and therefore many branches should be provided for it in a home vivarium. The Mangrove Snake requires a high degree of humidity, and the vivarium should be sprayed with lukewarm water twice a week and have an adequate water dish — even though this may seldom be seen to be used. Mangrove Snakes are very sensitive to light, hardly ever moving in the daytime ; many specimens will feed only in total darkness. Food requirements consist of rodents and small birds. The substitution of a dark-blue bulb may assist keepers who wish to ensure that the animal is indeed feeding.

Lizards

There are probably more species of lizard than of snakes, and certainly the variety of forms is much greater. Lizards range from the small *Amphibaenids*, which resemble earthworms, to the larger Dragons from the island of Komodo. Neither of these is suitable for the home vivarium, but many species are ideal, some even being capable of showing some affection. Many are simple to keep, and few inspire the repugnance often associated with snakes.

The possession of limbs is the most evident difference between lizards and snakes, yet there are some lizards — notably skinks — whose limbs are either non-existent or merely vestigial. Lizards invariably have eyelids, always absent in snakes, who have a single eye scale. In order to move, snakes have large belly scales across the width of the body which are attached to the ribs. Lizards have separate scales.

There are only two species of poisonous lizard, unlike the 200 or so venomous snakes. They are the members of the genus *Heloderma*, species *horridum* and *suspectum*. They do not have the more specialised poison glands and hollow fangs found in snakes, merely modified salivary glands, and poison is released into the mouth through a chewing motion — they do not strike at all.

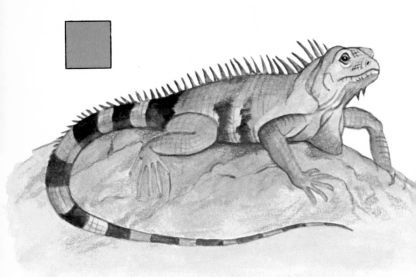

American Green Iguana *Iguana iguana*

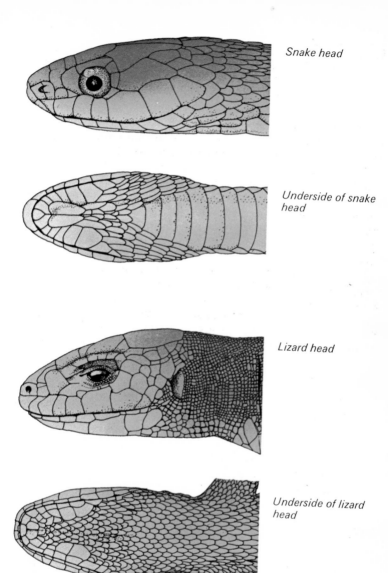

Snake head

Underside of snake head

Lizard head

Underside of lizard head

Among the differences between snakes and lizards are the absence of an eyelid in snakes and the large underside scales attached to their ribs: most lizards have eyelids and their scales are separate.

41

Giant Zonure *Cordylus giganteus*

The first lizard acquired is usually a small, indigenous specimen, although these are not really suited to life in the vivarium. South American Green Iguanas (*Iguana iguana*) are often purchased since they are beautiful to look at, fairly docile, and eat mainly vegetation: as they thrive only on fresh leaves, flowers, and fruit, however, they are not entirely happy in a vivarium. The authors began with specimens of a small family of lizards from South Africa — the Zonures. Some thirty species exist, all in the same genus (*Cordylus*), and all have a fairly similar appearance with a broad triangular head, slightly rough scales, and a spiny, well-armoured tail. Diversity within the family is limited to size, colour, and armour, the largest being the Giant Zonure, Sun Grazer, or Lord Derby's Girdled Lizard (*C. giganteus*), which grows up to one foot four inches long and will eat mice, rodents, and small birds, although most zonures feed only on insects, and other small invertebrates.

The smallest of the family is the Jones Zonure (*C. jonesii*), an adult being approximately two inches long. Like all zonures this species is oviparous, giving birth to live young (though sometimes youngsters about half an inch long, may be encased at birth in a thin membrane). Almost all zonures breed well in captivity, and many of the specimens imported from South Africa are pregnant females.

Girdle-tailed Lizard *Cordylus warreni*

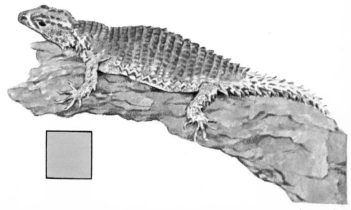

Furnishing a vivarium for zonures is little trouble. Basic essentials are a good floor, a shallow water dish, and a few large flat stones that will be used either as basking places during the day, or as retreats at night. Some species are more flattened in body shape than others and are able to squeeze themselves into very small spaces under stones. Apparent absence does not mean they have escaped; they will still need food and warmth. It is possible that they may hide in this way for several days when first deposited in the vivarium. Escapes are unlikely, but a check under the rocks does no harm unless they are carelessly replaced. Branches are not needed for zonures, since they are rock dwellers, but they will climb the sides, if at all rough, of any vivarium, so any gap at all beneath the lid offers a possible exit. In captivity, food supplied should be mealworms, wood lice, crickets, grasshoppers, or locusts. Many zonures become tame enough to feed from the hand, and a few will, with careful practice, become tame enough to be carried around clinging to their owner's pockets.

Geckos are often kept as pets, but not in a vivarium. In most areas where they are native they are encouraged to enter dwelling houses in order to catch the flying insects abundant in tropical and sub-tropical climates. Geckos are interesting to keep but have one drawback. Although they soon become accustomed to humans and will come to be fed regularly, as in the wild, they are accomplished escapologists and can climb up the smoothest, even glass, surfaces. Great care must be taken in setting up their home — even aquaria offer too many possibilities of escape. In designing the vivarium one should consider the animal's habits: if disturbed they run upwards to hide, so that a lid is no good. A door at the bottom of a side, allowing a secure area at the top of the vivarium, is necessary. The door must of course be close fitting — probably a sliding one is best. Any ventilation apertures must be covered at least with perforated zinc or muslin. Since geckos are insectivorous, living mainly on flies, the method by which the reptile-keeper feeds his charges has a bearing on the covering of the ventilators. If flies are to be placed in the vivarium then the covering should be fine enough to prevent their own escape. Alternatively a good food supply can be maintained by using a wider mesh through which flies, but not geckos, can pass. If a piece of meat or ripe fruit is provided, flies will be attracted into the vivarium and the geckos can eat their fill.

Since many geckos are arboreal the vivarium will require branches for climbing. Like most such lizards, geckos will lick up dew rather

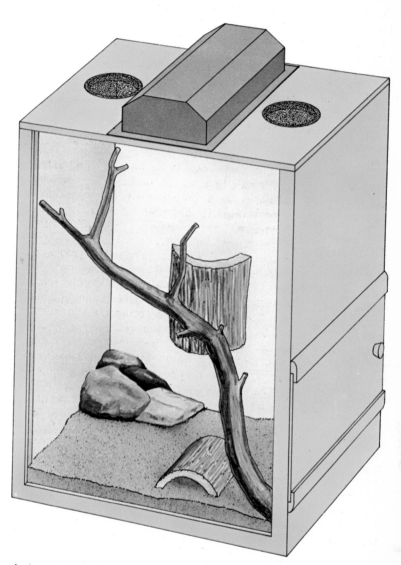

A vivarium for geckos should be constructed so that they can retreat to the top part of the cage, and a close-fitting sliding door should be at the bottom of one of the sides. If nocturnal geckos are being kept, they will respond more readily if a blue light is fitted.

45

Green Gecko *Phelsuwa niadagascariensis*

than drink, so no water container is necessary so long as the vivarium is sprayed daily with fresh soft water from a house-plant spray. Most geckos are nocturnal, coming out at twilight, though the bright-green members of the genus *Phelsuma*, the Day Geckos from Madagascar, are fond of daylight. The nocturnal majority respond more readily if their vivarium is equipped with a blue light.

Agamas agamas is a large family of lizards from Africa, Asia, and Australia, members of which frequently find their way into vivaria: there are far too many species to enumerate here, some being up to a yard in length, some only a matter of inches. Certain agamas have the ability to change colour to some extent, a good example being the Indian Changeable Lizard, or 'Bloodsucker'. It does not really suck blood, but in the mating season the male will turn bright red about the throat and chest as part of a threatening display similar to that found in birds and fish.

Agamas may require rocks to climb on, sand to burrow in, or 'trees' to hide in, so it is wise at first to provide a mixed set-up to see what a particular animal prefers and then increase the amount of his favourite cover. Above all agamas require space, especially when in contact with humans; it is commonplace for agamas to damage snouts, heads, and tails by running around trying to escape from too-small vivaria. An approximate guide might be that the run should be a minimum ten times the length of the inmates them-

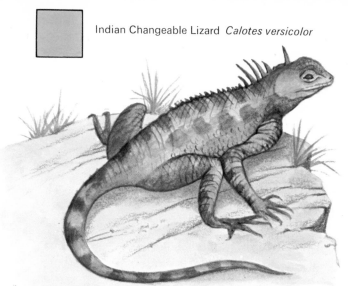

Indian Changeable Lizard *Calotes versicolor*

selves. Many agamas can withstand a high temperature, but they will require a pool in which to bathe and cool off. The pool, a shallow dish for preference, should not be placed directly under the heat, otherwise the water will evaporate too soon and the temperature of the remainder become excessive.

Most members of this family have very good teeth, which are fixed to the skull, and even the smallest species can bite fiercely. Their food depends upon size and habitat, some being very specialised: for example, the Australian *Moloch horridus* feeds only on ants. Most small agamids will take insect prey, but the larger species have no trouble with small birds and mammals, or even reptiles smaller than themselves — because of this large and small agamids do not co-exist peacefully.

Agamas are oviparous and may well mate and lay eggs in the vivarium. If mating is seen and the female begins to swell, it is time to prepare a maternity cage, since she will want to bury her eggs in the correct medium. Suitable media include sphagnum moss, peat, sand, vermiculite, or clean dry earth. Ideally, the pregnant female should be placed in a vivarium containing an assortment of media, so she can make her own choice. The choice of dry or damp remains: the expectant mother will determine this, if necessary, by urinating over the nest of eggs. It is therefore essential to provide her with drinking water.

IGUANAS

In the New World the equivalent of the agama is the iguana. Some members of the family are almost indistinguishable, while others differ, particularly in respect of diet. Several small agamids and some other small lizards such as cordylids will eat vegetation, but exist mainly on animal foods. However, many iguanas live mainly on vegetation, taking meat merely as an extra. One species, the Galapagos Marine Iguana, exists on a highly specialised diet of seaweed. It is reassuring to note that it is the larger iguanas which are the vegetarians.

A large vivarium is necessary for the iguana, preferably one big enough to accommodate the growing of plants. The fresher the food, the healthier the iguanas, which will be at their happiest when plucking tomatoes off the plant, or tearing lettuces from the ground. Although advantageous, this type of market gardening is not essential. However, sunlight is especially necessary for iguanas — the more they experience, the better their general condition. No vivarium should be placed in front of a window and left in the sun, though; it is better for it to be in a light room, facing a window, so that some sunshine falls on the specimen at some time during the day.

Stout branches will be required for an iguana, since all but desert species are expert climbers. Make sure that one branch is over the large water dish, as wild iguanas will bask on a branch overhanging a river or stream, diving into the water at the least sign of danger.

A feeding bowl is necessary unless growing vegetation is provided, or else food will be trodden into the floor covering. Disagreement exists among reptile keepers as to how vegetable matter should be served. Finely chopped food is advocated by some owners, while others point out that this is not available in the wild, and that whole plants should therefore be given. This argument is countered by the assertion that plants should be rooted into the ground, so that an animal can bite and pull off pieces which could not so easily be separated from a plant lying on the floor of a vivarium. A compromise would lie in cutting the food, be it lettuce, tomatoes, cauliflower, Brussels sprouts, or fruit, into bite-sized pieces — leaving perhaps one or two large leaves to be eaten at the reptile's leisure. A little chopped meat should be added twice a week, and the diet can also be varied by a twice-weekly addition of a few mealworms or slugs. The food bowl should be cleaned and replenished every day.

The smaller, non-vegetarian iguanas should be fed as if they were

Galapagos Marine Iguana
Amblyrhynchus cristatus

agamas, with a mixed insect diet such as spiders, crickets, beetles, mealworms, woodlice, and flies. Slightly larger specimens may take small mice and birds, but if they are over one foot three inches, the specimens are probably vegetarian.

Iguanas are oviparous reptiles, but unlike agamas the iguanids do not breed so well in the vivarium. As with all groups of lizards, when more than one young iguana is housed in a vivarium, a watch should be kept to ensure that all inmates are able to feed satisfactorily. Dominant individuals may frighten off weaker specimens, resulting in adverse effects calling for the construction of a natural screen with several feeding dishes. The screen should be rigid and of a neutral colour to ensure that the reptiles are not put off their food altogether. During observation unnecessary noise and movement should be minimised, since most reptiles, especially snakes and lizards, will not feed if frightened. The keeper will find it interesting to watch reptiles feeding and, as with all animals, this is the first step towards taming.

A Linnean Iguana in a perfect vivarium setting

Skinks

Skinks are the most widespread of all lizards, being found in Europe, Africa, Asia, Australia, and America. Few grow very large, most being between four inches and one foot in length. All skinks are ground-living reptiles; some only have rudimentary limbs and some are legless, but most are burrowers — this is reflected in the skin, the scales of which are small and close together. There are few appendages such as crests on their cylindrical or flattened bodies, but members of the genus *Eumeces* have fringes or flaps of skin which cover the ears when the animal burrows.

The important aspect of vivarium furnishing for skinks is the floor-covering, the majority of the family being content with approximately one inch of sand, so long as a few rocks are provided for basking. A water dish is unnecessary — few skinks can tolerate damp — but a little water should be sprayed on the ground in the morning. Their tastes in food are wide, including insects, lettuce, fruit, cooked meat or egg, preferably chopped up. Some of the

Stumped-tailed Skink *Trachydosaurus rugosus*

larger skinks may take small birds or mammals, but it is not common. Skinks are livebearers, and as with other viviparous reptiles breeding is fairly easy. This is an advantage as some of the larger skinks from Australia are now difficult to obtain outside that country, including the Shingleback or Two-headed Lizard, common names for the stump-tailed skink, whose head is shaped like its tail both to confound enemies and to contain reserves of fatty tissue. Another Australian species popular in the vivarium is the Blue-tongued Skink, the aptness of whose name becomes clear when it is seen licking up dew in the vivarium.

Blue-tongued Skink also called Giant Skink (USA) *Tiliqua scincoides*

Lacertids

The *lacertids* are the *forma typica* of lizards. They conform to the popular image of the lizard and are often found in vivaria. Europe, North Africa, and the temperate zones of Asia are the natural homes of these fairly small lizards, and as with most animals from temperate climates they are not as brightly coloured as their tropical counterparts, though none the less interesting to keep. Few need so much heat, but while they must not be allowed to get cold, they can withstand greater variations in temperature. In natural surroundings the ambient temperature may not be high, but the places inhabited, such as walls, rocks, and under heather often provide a climate of a rather hotter kind.

The vivarium need not be large but should be fairly well ventilated. This will probably allow greater heat loss than with a tropical arrangement, so the specimens will not be inconvenienced by a normal lamp — a full heater lamp should not be necessary. High humidity is not essential, but neither should the vivarium be as arid as a desert. A water dish should be provided for drinking, but bathing is unlikely. The floor can be left bare, but dry leaves, peat, or moss are preferable to gravel. Rocks, branches, and tree bark, as provided for agamas, will be used by most lacertids, who require a similar food supply — insects, flies, larvae, and slugs for the majority, with mice and birds for the larger green and the jewelled or eyed lizards. The latter, found around the Mediterranean and probably the most beautiful of lacertids, do well in captivity. The green lizard, however, commonly sold by European reptile dealers, is not ideally suited for vivaria, since sunlight plays such an important part in its assimilation of essential vitamins that it should really be kept in an outside terrarium or in a greenhouse where natural sunlight is available. The specimen or specimens — it is preferable to keep a group — will still require the same feeding, while the provision of a dish of mealworms or earthworms can form the basis of a rapport between the reptile-keeper and his semi-wild animals. The appearance of dark-brown 'warts' on a lizard is the initial sign that it is not enjoying sufficient sunlight. This should be remedied at once; if other suitable accommodation is not available the specimen should be released, provided it has not become too weak.

Hibernation is also an important consideration when keeping lacertids. Species from more northerly latitudes will hibernate, or go into a state of dormancy, for up to seven months of the year. It is difficult to cater for hibernation in the vivarium, since it is no straight forward matter. Any hibernating animal will build up a reserve of food about its body, while some mammals will build a home for the period of hibernation. The herpetologist keeping such creatures should at least be able to vary considerably the temperature in the vivarium. This is not merely a case of substituting a

Jewelled or Eyed Lizard *Lacerta lepida*

Green Lizard *Lacerta viridis*

weaker light-bulb, there must be an accurate control built into the power circuit so that a gradual reduction of heat can be obtained.

Preparation for hibernation should begin in August in the Northern Hemisphere, when the heater is left at the lower night temperature for longer periods, the time being increased by fifteen minutes every week. More food should be provided to enable the specimens to build up the reserves of fatty tissue, and a wooden box containing dry peat and leaves should be introduced into the vivarium at this time, providing a hibernaculum — a place where reptiles hibernate. Some of the other cover should be removed to encourage the use of the box. At the end of August the daytime temperature can be decreased very gradually and the specimens should respond by consuming more food. The temperature at which a reptile hibernates will depend upon its species and its home locality. Some adders have been seen on snow for short periods and American snapping turtles have been sighted swimming in iced-over ponds.

The vivarium specimen should soon settle down in a box, and it is quite normal for several to hibernate in one place; in the wild, adders, rattlesnakes, and many lacertids do so. When all the individuals have settled down in the box it can be gently removed and placed somewhere cold and draught-free, such as a cellar or cupboard under stairs. The box should be covered securely, to prevent rats getting at and eating the reptiles, and then left undisturbed until the spring. In March it should be brought out and placed in the vivarium, initially unheated. When the specimens wake the heat should be switched on and raised to normal living temperature straight away and food and warm water immediately made available. Some hibernating reptiles die when they wake because the weather is insufficiently warm for them to feed. On no account should the reptiles be disturbed during hibernation.

This method of assisting the hibernation of reptiles is suitable for snakes and tortoises as well as lizards, but should not be attempted in the case of alligators. So little is known about alligator hibernation that it would be quite wrong for the amateur to experiment.

Returning to lizards, in the Americas the place of the lacertid is taken by the family known as *Teiids*. There are some 200 species in this family, and generally they should be treated as lacertidae when kept in the vivarium. An exception to this principle is genus *Tupinambis*, the tegu, a large lizard up to one yard in length that can be both lively and vicious. Similar to the monitor lizard or varanid of the Old World, the tegu is reared in just the same way.

Monitors

A vivarium for tegus or monitors must be large and strong with sparse internal furnishing. A long vivarium is preferable and there must be a large water dish or small pool in which the inmates can bathe. Heating is crucial. Both types of lizard have a high metabolic rate, and are more susceptible to cold than others. One yard is a reasonable size for a tegu, though less than average for many monitors, the largest of which is the Komodo Dragon which grows up to twelve feet in length. All are equipped with powerful claws and teeth and a dangerous whip-like tail. It may be prudent when constructing a vivarium for a large monitor or tegu to provide two separate lids, at each end, rather than have the whole upper surface capable of being lifted. The lids must have catches to match the animal's strength, and should be large enough to allow easy access for servicing, so that all parts of the vivarium can be reached from one end or the other. Having two lids makes possible the cleaning of one end while the lizard is in the other end — if the specimen is very aggressive it may be necessary to hold it at bay with a stick, or place a barrier across the vivarium, to prevent attack or escape. While this would be an extreme measure, one should not expect such creatures to be playful pets.

There should be nothing in the vivarium that the lizards can dislodge with their strong tails. A plain painted-wood floor is best, with a large plastic water bowl which if possible should be flush with the floor, so that it cannot be burrowed under or tipped up. A large piece of cork-bark will serve as cover and as a basking spot; nothing else is necessary. Vivaria with considerably more decoration can be seen in zoos, but these are likely to be cleaned every day, a considerable chore for the amateur voluntarily to set himself.

Feeding monitors and tegus is simple — fresh-killed meat, meat from a butcher, or eggs, and preferably all three, make a good diet. These lizards will accept cold raw meat more readily than most reptiles, especially if a raw egg is broken over it, but fresh-killed mice, rats, or voles are consumed with even greater relish. Small birds, such as day-old chicks and pigeons are also suitable if the animal is up to a yard long, though over this size the food should be more substantial (for example, rabbits, hares, or chickens). In extreme cases, young deer, calves, and pigs would be the only suitable fodder for the Komodo Dragon, the Perenty from Australia, and the Water Monitor from Asia. These creatures are rarely found in private collections, however, the usual representatives of the *Varanidae* being the Nile Monitor (*Varanus niloticus*) and the

Komodo Dragon *Varanus komodoensis*

The correct way to pick up a Monitor

Bosc's or Savannah Monitor from Africa. Many species exist, varying mainly in size and colour, but all should be treated with equal respect. The only way to pick up a monitor is from above, one hand behind the head and one over the back just in front of the back legs, with the tail tucked under the arm. Any specimen over four feet six inches long should be handled by two people.

Monitors are similar to snakes in a number of ways. The tongue is forked, and the gait is much like the lateral undulations of most snakes. Monitors are in fact the lizards most closely related to snakes, in spite of the fact that one group of lizards has no limbs and is called the snake lizard, or *Anguidae*; the Slow Worm and Glass Snake are members of this family. That the tongue is not forked, the presence of eyelids, and the ventral scales all demonstrate that these are lizards, and should be treated as such. Slow worms and glass snakes, or *scheltopusiks*, are commonly kept; the slow worm is a smaller version of the latter, feeding on insects, slugs and earthworms, while the *scheltopusik* feeds on small mammals, frogs, and birds. In the vivarium it will be satisfied with mice and day-old chicks, and a water dish and plenty of cover are necessary. These reptiles should be kept not hot but merely warm, and should be allowed to hibernate as they would do in the wild.

Chameleons

Formerly classified as a group of reptiles separate from lizards, they are now acknowledged only to be a specialised form. Their often exaggerated ability to change colour is the most well-known characteristic of eighty-five species of chameleon. It will by now be clear that the ability to change colour is not unique to chameleons, but there are nevertheless several peculiarities distinguishing them from other reptiles. Each side of a chameleon is governed by an independent nervous system, so that the eyes by swivelling around in their sockets can transmit two separate images to the brain. When something of interest is seen by either eye, that takes over while the other swivels to focus on the same object, giving binocular vision. The chameleon decides whether it is food or an enemy; if food, the creature will gently move into range and catch it with its extending tongue. The feet are bifurcated — that is to say that the digits are opposed in two groups, on each side of the branch to which the chameleon is clinging. All chameleons live in trees and bushes, whether they be the dwarf species of a few inches or the larger ones of up to two feet. They also have prehensile tails which are never shed.

Unsuited to life in vivaria, chameleons never thrive in captivity. They need live insects, mainly flies, and plenty of sunlight. They have been kept successfully in greenhouses, probably the best place for them, but some herpetologists prefer to leave chameleons outside on a small tree or bush throughout the summer — naturally a sunny spot is essential. Surprisingly the animals seem to flourish, being able to accommodate themselves to a drop in temperature at night so long as the daytime temperature reaches 26°C. Birds may be a danger, in which case the bush should be enclosed in the netting used by gardeners to protect fruit and flowers; it may then be necessary to place bait, such as rotting fruit or meat, to attract more flies.

During the winter the chameleons will have to be brought inside the house, or into a greenhouse. In either case the best home for them is a large, twiggy branch suspended from the ceiling by very thin twine, or fishing line, which they cannot climb. A heater lamp can be placed near to them in daytime, unless the room is in any case reasonably warm — between 16°C and 21°C. Food can be obtained by purchasing maggots or gentles, the larvae of the house fly, which are sold as bait for fishing. If a few at a time are presented in a dish of sawdust they will metamorphose into flies in the warmth, and can be snapped up by the chameleon. Only the experience of a

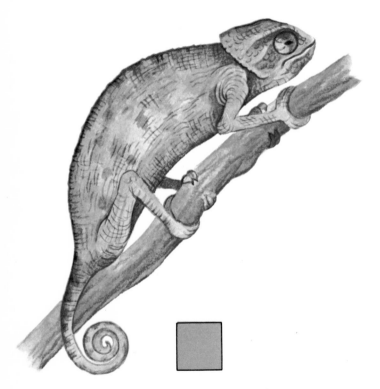

Mediterranean Chameleon *Chameleo vulgaris*

particular arrangement can determine the number of gentles that will satisfy your reptile without creating swarms of flies. Naturally, fly sprays must never be used near chameleons or other insect-eating reptiles, since the poison that kills the flies will accumulate in the body of the reptile and before long cause its death too. Swarms of flies can be dealt with by using sticky fly papers that will catch the insects without hurting the reptile.

Crocodilians

There are three groups of crocodilians in the world today — the true crocodiles, the alligators and caymans, and the gavial. Crocodiles are most widespread, inhabiting Asia, Africa, Madagascar, Australia, and both North and South America. The alligators, represented by two species, come from North America and China, whereas the caymans are restricted to South America and the West Indies. The gavial, or gharial, is the sole member of its family and is found only in India and Burma.

All crocodiles are perfectly adapted to their amphibious existence. The characteristic elongated snout terminates in a rather bulbous nose with the nostrils right on top. The eyes are placed high on the head, so that the reptile can swim just below the surface of the water with just its eyes and nostrils visible. The tongue of the crocodilian fits neatly across the back of the throat, permitting fast underwater pursuit of prey with the jaws open, without the risk of drowning. When walking on land the crocodilian raises itself well off the ground by its legs, but these are not employed when swimming; when travelling at speed in water they are held flat against the body and propulsion is achieved solely with the muscular, vertically-flattened tail.

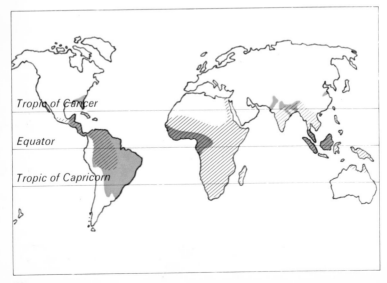

Food is seized by a lightning snap of the tooth-studded jaws and is swallowed whole, the reptile's head being raised clear of the water during the movement. When larger prey is seized the crocodilian rapidly twists its body over and over, thus tearing the unfortunate victim apart. Usually, however, crocodilians restrict themselves to easily-managed food, basically fish, small mammals, and birds.

Eggs are laid in a rough mound of mud and decaying vegetation, and are vigilantly attended by the female during incubation. On hatching, the female breaks up the nest and the young scurry off to the nearest water, where they begin to feed almost immediately upon aquatic invertebrates and small fish and amphibians. Growth is rapid and may reach one or two feet a year for the first six or seven years of life.

Juvenile crocodilians are perhaps the most appealing and interesting of vivarium inhabitants, although their rapid growth and fierce temperament present serious problems to the amateur herpetologist. Unfortunately, the South American Cayman (*Caiman crocodilus*) has in the last few years been ruthlessly exploited through the pet trade, and thousands of newly hatched babies are sold to the general public as 'baby alligators'. Very few of these survive more than a few weeks of captivity, simply because their

Key

Crocodiles – Genus *Crocodylus*

African dwarf crocodiles – *Osteolaemus tetraspis*

Alligators – Genus *Alligator*

False gavial – *Tomistoma schlegeli*

Gavial – *Gavial gangeticus*

Caymans – Genera *Caiman, Melanosuchus, Paleosuchus*

Crocodiles, alligators, caymans, and the gavial are found mainly in inland waters, such as lakes, rivers, swamps, and estuaries. The majority live within the Tropics.

Cayman Paraguayan or Jacare Cayman (USA) *Caiman yacare*

Spectacled Cayman *Caiman crocodilus*

Mississippi Alligator *Alligator mississippiensis*

owners are ignorant as to their diet and temperature requirements. Those few that persist are usually dumped on a local zoo when, after a couple of years, their increased size has made them unmanagable. Taking on a young crocodilian is a task requiring careful thought, particularly with regard to the accommodation of the adult specimen. Largely as a result of indiscriminate hunting for their skins, most species in the order have become rare in their natural environment and anyone keeping them in captivity therefore has an obligation to do so properly.

Only a limited number of species are available to the private collector, the cayman being the most commonly imported one. It reaches an adult length of about six feet and while it may be docile when young it usually becomes intractable with maturity. The bite of any crocodilian can be a serious and unpleasant experience, so great care should be taken especially when handling one whose

West-African Dwarf Crocodile   *Osteolamus tetraspis tetraspis*

temperament is unknown. The best strategy is to pick it up gently and firmly behind the head with one hand, supporting the body with the other. In cases where the specimen is large it is necessary to trap the tail against your body with your arm. Animals over a yard long are better handled by two people — the strength of a crocodilian even of this meagre size being unbelievable! Occasionally available, the Dwarf or Smooth-Fronted Cayman (*Paleosuchus palpebrosus*), with its average adult length of little more than a yard is perhaps the most practical proposition for the amateur.

Undoubtedly the most suitable 'pet' in this order is the Mississippi Alligator (*Alligator mississippiensis*), from the swamps of southeastern North America. Although growing rapidly and frequently exceeding lengths of ten feet, the young animal is suited to vivarium life because of its placidity and hardiness. Unfortunately this species has virtually disappeared from the wild because its skin is thought valuable, but thanks to vigorous protective measures by the US government it is now on the increase once more. Obviously this species is not commonly on sale; those specimens that are sold have normally been in captivity for some years, and command a high price.

Crocodiles (genus *Crocodylus*) such as the Nile, Estuarine, and Siamese, are sometimes imported but rarely kept by private collectors because of the fierce temper and excessive size of the mature beast. The West African Dwarf Crocodile (*Osteolamus tetraspis tetraspis*) rarely grows to more than five feet and is therefore much more suitable.

Housing
Crocodilians, when very small, can be housed in an aquarium tank with a small land area, as mentioned in the chapter on vivarium management. A relatively high temperature of 27°C to 29°C is needed for both land and water areas, as young crocodilians are more prone to chills than any other reptile.

When his charges have outgrown the aquarium, the herpetologist must consider whether he wants to keep them or donate them to a zoo — most zoos with reptile collections seem to accumulate unwanted crocodilians and so would be unlikely to pay for any of the commoner species. If the specimens are retained then a pool in a greenhouse or shed offers suitable accommodation, though the cost of its elaborate and expensive heating requirements should be borne in mind. Radiation from heat bulbs will be insufficient to warm a large pen and powerful immersion heaters will have to be installed in the pool; these must have a guard of some kind to prevent them being broken by the crocodilian. Heating the land area can best be achieved either by radiators or a thermostatically controlled fan heater, but all electrical appliances should be kept away from the inmates, and their sometimes vigourous splashing must be prevented from causing damage. Crocodilians of approximately the same size can be kept together, even though they may be of different species. Sometimes, however, fighting may occur, and the reptile responsible should be removed. Care is needed at feeding time to ensure that the crocodilians do not fight over the same piece of food.

Feeding

Unfortunately the majority of captive crocodilians receive as their basic diet nothing more than raw meat. These reptiles, being so prone to rickets, must be fed on a diet containing an abundance of calcium and natural roughage. Small specimens may be fed on chopped sprats, mice, and chicken, graduating to whole sprats and mice as the creatures grow. Specimens three or four feet long can easily take herrings and rats.

Frequency of feeds depends on the appetite of the individual, but on alternate days is probably the best feeding routine. Food must be placed in the water, as few specimens will eat on land; those which refuse to eat can usually be tempted by waving the morsel on a light rod to the side of the jaws of the crocodile. If he snaps and seizes the food, the likelihood is that he will swallow it.

Attention to the cleanliness of the pool is important, all uneaten food being removed after an hour or so.

Chelonians

The chelonians are the group of reptiles that carry their homes with them: the tortoises, also known as turtles or terrapins. They are the most commonly kept of all reptiles. Few people have not touched or been near a tortoise at some time in their lives, yet the same people would often recoil at even the thought of contact with other reptiles. Many more books have been written on keeping tortoises than on other reptiles, so here the emphasis will be on the more exotic species.

A vivarium is not so necessary for a chelonian, and certainly not for land tortoises. Water tortoises, or terrapins, will do better in an aquarium, and marine turtles will live only in a heated salt-water aquarium — beyond the resources of most amateur collectors. The tortoises are distinguished from terrapins and turtles by having feet rather than flippers, and the legs are stumpy with a flattened sole.

Naturally, the shell of a chelonian restricts its movements somewhat, and few are any good at climbing unless a gentle slope or plenty of footholds are available, so a low wall is all that is necessary to contain a tortoise. The smaller the specimen the more readily will it climb, but a reasonable barrier would be twice the creature's own height. An area of a yard square should be enough for any specimen up to four inches long, more for larger specimens, in the same ratio. This of course would represent a permanent home, but since a tortoise can safely be allowed more freedom than most reptiles, many keepers allow their pets to wander at liberty over a room or garden, returning it to its home at night. This is quite reasonable so long as everybody is aware of the tortoise's presence — it cannot get out of the way quickly.

Food is always some kind of vegetation, and anything can be repeatedly offered as long as it is consumed. However, no creature should be restricted to a diet of lettuce or cabbage and nothing else, since all need calcium for healthy growth of the shell. Cuttlefish bone or broken eggshell should be powdered and sprinkled over the food regularly. Water is usually absorbed from the food, but a shallow dish should be provided for the occasional drink and bath, the dish requiring gently sloping sides so that the specimen can get out should it climb in. A dish should be provided for holding the food and this should be cleaned everyday to prevent uneaten food going rotten.

All tortoises should be kept at a temperature of at least 19°C, but more heat will be needed for the species coming from tropical climates, whether desert or jungle ; a simple electric lamp suspended from above the enclosure will be sufficient in most cases. Any tortoise will do better if allowed out in the sunshine to eat fresh vegetation whenever the opportunity arises.

Common Tortoises

Terrapins

Terrapins are native to all continents except Antarctica, and none is found far from water which is usually fresh, although some terrapins live in tidal estuaries or brackish swamps. Two schools of thought exist with regard to the care of terrapins. One suggests that they live in sparkling clear water which is changed frequently, and always within a few hours of food being offered or droppings deposited. The alternative viewpoint suggests that terrapins thrive in thick green water choked with algae and weed. Evaluation of either view is difficult, and possibly individual species or even specimens may have different tastes. In general the dirty water method will only succeed in an outdoor pool; in the confines of vivarium or aquarium, clean water should always be used.

An aquarium is essential for terrapins. Gravel and vegetation can be dispensed with, the only necessary furnishing being a large stone to provide a basking area — a piece of broken paving slab is ideal. Only one stone should be used, and should be positioned to

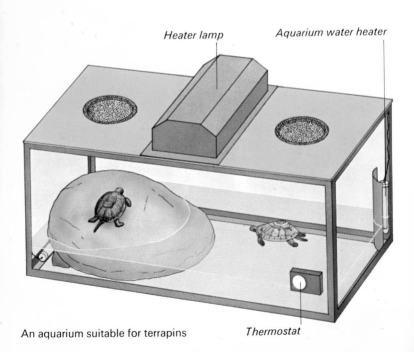

Heater lamp   Aquarium water heater

An aquarium suitable for terrapins   *Thermostat*

slope gently into the water. The stone should also be firm, so that the lively terrapins cannot dislodge it and either break the glass of their home or become trapped underneath; such accidents are a common cause of fatalities among captive terrapins. Some herpetologists prefer to use a piece of wood floating on the water, but terrapins may encounter difficulty in climbing onto such an island, and unless it is large they will never be able to dry out completely.

Plastic bowls complete with plastic palm trees are sometimes offered for sale, but these are quite useless. They are too small other than for hatching terrapins and have no provision for the heating system that is vital to any terrapin small enough to live therein.

There is considerable trade in the American Red-Eared terrapin (*Pseudemys scripta elegans*), usually offered for sale at about an inch long. Most die soon after purchase since they need a temperature of at least 24°C, and they *do* grow to a length of over a foot, despite the protests of most vendors to the contrary.

American Red-eared Terrapin *Pseudemys scripta elegans*

Anybody in Europe who wishes to keep terrapins can do no better than to start with the European Pond Tortoise (*Emys obicularis*). These are hardy terrapins which hibernate in winter and could be kept in a garden pool, providing it has a mud bottom, as easily as in any aquarium. They can be left out in a pool all the year round, experiencing no discomfort during a reasonably mild winter. A Red-eared Terrapin over six inches long could be kept in the same way, providing it has grown to that size in its natural habitat. An aquarium-raised specimen would not be strong enough to endure the rigours of the climate.

Returning to the terrapin in the aquarium, a thermometer should be used to check the water temperature regularly, but it is dangerous to leave an ordinary one in the water permanently as it will soon get broken. An aquarium thermometer is preferable, adhering to the outside of the tank and giving a reading based on heat transmitted through the glass side. Should the temperature drop below 15°C, the water will need to be reheated. A normal aquarium heater placed behind the basking rock, or in a protective container of perforated zinc, should be satisfactory. Possibly it would be preferable to site this and the thermostat in the angle between the sides and on the floor of the tank, but this principle can be adapted according to the conditions of a particular set-up. Sometimes the tank can be heated from above if the strength of a light-bulb is deemed sufficient. The bulb need not be particularly powerful, but it should be high above the water, since drops of water splashing it when hot will soon shatter it and then the specimens would suffer from their ensuing exposure to cold and broken glass. The depth of water need not be great, but twice the height of the inmates would be a minimum; if terrapins cannot submerge completely their shells will become too dry and begin to flake off.

Food for terrapins is not dried like fish food, nor is it raw meat or fish. They require whole organisms, such as small fish, earthworms, and water snails complete with shells, together with a little lettuce or water weed. No small fish with spines, such as stickleback or miller's thumb, should be given — the spines are to protect the fish from being eaten, and a terrapin driven by hunger to try them will soon be suffering from a wounded mouth. Daphnia and tubifex sold for aquarists will be enjoyed by most young terrapins, who will have great fun chasing the former.

There are several terrapins which require special treatment. The soft-shelled species have a leathery, rather than bony, shell, and are not suitable for housing with other terrapins who will nibble away

European Pond Tortoises *Emys obicularis*

at the edge of the shell. Instead they should be kept on their own in an aquarium with a floor-covering of fine sand in which they will burrow. These terrapins need calcium as much as other chelonians; there is no need to reduce or adapt their food supply simply because of their unusual shells.

The Snapping Turtles from North America must also be isolated, as they are both vicious and powerful. There are two species each

North American Snapping Turtles *Chelydra serpentina*

Alligator Snapping Turtle *Macrochelys temmincki*

Mata-Mata Turtle *Chelys fimbriata*

of its own genus. The Common Snapping Turtle (*Chelydra serpentina*) is more commonly found in captivity and grows to approximately one foot four inches. The Alligator Snapper (*Macrochelys temmincki*) is larger and comes from the south-west of North America. Both are rather ugly, but their form offers good camouflage in their natural environment. Both will snap at anything moving near their heads, and the latter has a filament visible when its mouth is left agape, which lures small fish to their doom. No land space need be provided in the aquarium, as the snapper will not use it, and providing the site is in a room of normal, equitable living temperature only the smallest specimens, under three inches, will require any artificial heating. Whole fish, mice, and chicks are acceptable as food, and as the specimen grows so the size of its meals can be increased. The snapper, however, a slow-moving terrapin, must not be permitted to become obese, as this will prevent it achieving maturity, let alone longevity. Lastly, snappers should not be picked up with any part of the hand near the front half of the specimen, nor just by the tail. The former will hurt the collector, the latter the snapper!

An interesting terrapin occasionally available to the private collector is the Mata-mata (*Chelys fimbriata*) from Brazil and the Guyanas. Similar to the snappers in its dependence upon excellent camouflage, it is slow moving and totally aquatic. It is carnivorous like the snappers, but it grows neither so large nor so dangerous. The mata-mata is not fond of light, so it is better to heat the water rather than rely on radiant heat. A floor-covering of fine mud will be appreciated; the terrapin will burrow in it, and assisted by its excellent camouflage become almost undiscernible.

The true turtles which are found in tropical seas throughout the world are unsuitable for home aquaria. They need salt water, which would necessitate an all-glass or at least specially sealed aquarium tank, together with filtration equipment designed especially for the purpose. They also need to be kept warm, and a tank of flowing water is more expensive to heat than a normal static-water tank. Marine turtles are large and require a larger set-up than a terrapin or tortoise of similar size; since a turtle of one foot three inches long is normal — many grow far bigger — the size of the problem becomes apparent. Again, as these species are rare, due to the over-collecting of their eggs and to building developments on their breeding beaches, anyone considering keeping them should first read more extensively.

Ailments

Reptiles, like all living creatures, occasionally become ill. Unfortunately, very little research has been done on their diseases, or on possible treatments, and this puts the herpetologist at a disadvantage compared with the aquarist, who has dozens of remedies available to cope with likely diseases. The average veterinary surgeon is completely out of his depth when confronted with a sick reptile, simply because he is required to deal with a creature whose structure and metabolism is entirely different from those he has been trained to deal with. However, a good vet is an invaluable aid when it comes to the selection of drugs and the correct quantity required for a certain body weight.

The principle that 'prevention is better than cure' is an excellent guide when dealing with reptiles. If specimens are fed correctly and kept at the appropriate temperature in good, clean conditions, and care is taken not to introduce any disease-ridden recent acquisition into an established collection, then the risk of illness will be minimised.

Parasites: Both tapeworms and roundworms are found occasionally in captive reptiles, and are manifested in the infected specimen by a ravenous appetite, coupled with a failure to put on weight. Whole worms, or in the case of tapeworms, segments only, may be passed out in the droppings. Lungworms, which are found in the lungs and trachea, are fairly common in newly imported specimens, especially from Asia. The infected reptile wheezes and splutters, holds its mouth slightly open, and in severe cases the throat is distended.

Victims of worm infections must be isolated from the rest of the collection in order to prevent the spread of disease. Fortunately, worming cures used for mammals and birds are usually effective against reptilian parasites, and if a good vet is consulted a cure can often be found.

External parasites, in the shape of ticks and mites, frequently occur in newly imported stock and must be eradicated with all haste. Ticks, which are often found in snakes, lizards, and tortoises, are easy to spot, looking like small grey and black peas with legs. It is dangerous merely to pull these off, since the head will be buried in the reptile's skin and may break off from the body and continue to fester unnoticed. Rather, a tiny drop of paraffin should be applied to the tick, and in several seconds it will have relaxed itself instinctively and may be removed with a pair of forceps.

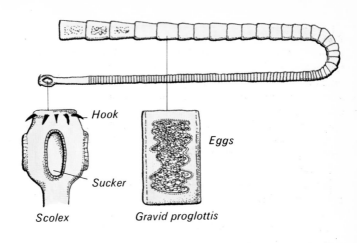

Hook

Eggs

Sucker

Scolex

Gravid proglottis

Lungworms   Oral sucker   Ventral sucker

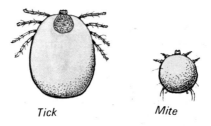

Tick   Mite

Parasites that can endanger the health of a reptile

Mites occasionally infect reptiles, especially snakes. They can do great damage by travelling at speed through an entire collection. Many remedies have been advocated, such as wiping victims with olive oil to suffocate the mites and their eggs, or leaving them confined in a container of tepid water for a day or two so that the mites are drowned. The vivarium must, in the meantime, be thoroughly disinfected and scalded several times to destroy any mites or eggs harbouring in the furnishings or in any cracks in the sides, top and bottom.

Fortunately a useful product has come onto the market in recent years consisting of a chemical strip which gives off vapours poisonous to insects. These, originally designed to rid domestic larders of flies, are ideal for eradicating and preventing mites in reptile collections — one should note, however, that there must be no possibility of the reptiles eating insects killed in this manner.

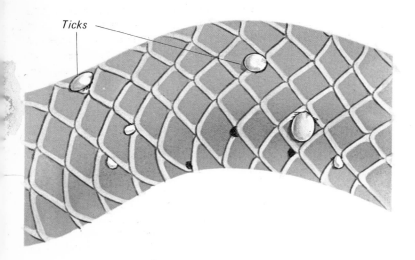

Ticks

Ticks are easy to spot, but they should not be merely pulled off the reptile. A little paraffin should first be applied.

Injuries and wounds: To some extent these can be prevented by making sure that specimens do not come into contact with broken glass or sharp surfaces, and by not mixing species or individuals which are known to fight. All flesh wounds should be cleaned with a mild antiseptic and dressed with a good powder or ointment.

Vitamin deficiencies: These are sadly all too common, particularly among chelonians and crocodilians which have been raised from birth in captivity. Tortoises and terrapins, if deprived of calcium, phosphates, and natural sunlight, develop soft or malformed shells, and in the latter stages swollen and constantly shut eyes. Crocodilians suffering similar deprivations lose their teeth, develop badly formed jaws, and lose the ability to walk on land. Should the herpetologist acquire a specimen suffering from avitaminoris he should treat it with a varied, calcium-rich diet, such as whole animals, water snails, etc. As much natural sunlight as possible should be available for basking in, and a carefully employed ultra-violet lamp would almost certainly be of benefit.

Colds and chills: These are caused either by subjecting the animals to sudden drops in temperature, or by keeping them at too low a temperature for a long period. Snakes and lizards thus treated sneeze and blow bubbles from their nostrils, whereas chelonians and crocodilians develop running eyes. Infected reptiles should be kept at a slightly higher temperature than is normal, and if the symptoms persist they must be dosed orally with a grain or two of sulphanilamide powder, or a small amount of aureomycin.

A reptile which arrives in a chilled, sluggish condition, as may well happen after a long train journey from a dealer, should immediately be placed in a warm vivarium at 30°C. Sometimes it is beneficial to give it an immediate bath in tepid water, taking care that it does not drown.

Growths and abscesses: Growths and abscesses are not uncommon, particularly in larger reptiles. Swellings occur under the skin, and these can be lanced and thoroughly cleaned out with luke-warm water and a mild antiseptic. The wound should be dressed with sulphanilamide powder or aureomycin.

Often the feet of vivarium inmates, especially large lizards such as tegus and monitors, swell up until the whole foot resembles a ball. The cause of this condition is unknown, though it is liable to be aggravated by the use of underfloor heating. A possible cure is an injection of the drug Tylan-50, which has been used effectively against the disease known as bumblefoot that sometimes attacks

poultry and birds of prey. But a veterinary surgeon should always be consulted as soon as possible.

The small blisters that affect water-snakes that have been kept in unsuitable, damp conditions are exceedingly difficult to cure. Supplying a bone-dry vivarium (except for drinking water), and swabbing the infected areas with antiseptic, may prove beneficial.

Mouth canker: Mouth canker, or mouth rot, is a particularly unpleasant scourge found among snakes and the larger lizards. An infected reptile develops a white, cheesy substance, which begins to spread around its jaws and later over the whole inner surface of the mouth and throat. Particles flake off and are swallowed and the disease spreads to the animal's internal organs with fatal results. In particularly severe cases the jaw rapidly rots away and the teeth drop out as the jawbone becomes infected. The reptile suffering in this way generally refuses to feed.

Periodic checks should be made on the mouths of captive reptiles, especially those undergoing a fast or those which persistently strike the glass of the vivarium. Any inflammation must be treated immediately with careful swabbings of mild, watered-down antiseptic. Should cankerous areas develop these must be picked off daily and the mouth's interior swabbed thoroughly. Application of an acriflavin-based cream is helpful. Treatment must continue until all trace of canker is gone. In severe cases, an intra-muscular injection of sulphamezathine, given by a veterinary surgeon, may help but will tend to affect the animal's kidneys. If employed, it is wise to see that the animal drinks all the water it can obtain. If a particular specimen drinks only infrequently, it must have water squirted down its throat periodically via a piece of tubing attached to a syringe.

Constipation: Many of the large boas and pythons are very inactive in captivity and are prone to get build-ups of faeces and urates in the intestine and bladder. A small dose of medicinal paraffin will help, but usually all that is needed is a little enforced exercise such as letting the specimen crawl freely round a room or allowing it to swim in a large container of water.

Peritonitis: Peritonitis is caused by damage to the wall of the gut, which thickens in the infected area and thus prevents recently swallowed food moving any further. The food then decomposes without being digested, killing the reptile. Unfortunately the first

symptom visible to the herpetologist is when a specimen suffering from peritonitis bloats out of all proportion to a meal it has just consumed. When this happens the creature's death is only a day or so away. Prey too large for a snake to swallow easily is a possible cause of gut rupture.

Vitamins: Many multi-vitamin preparations marketed for children and elderly people are also good for reptiles. Captive animals live in a totally artificial, man-made environment, where the variety of foods presented to them cannot be expected to compete with that available in the natural state. Vitamins in a liquid form may be injected into dead rodents and tablets can be finely crushed and mixed with the food of fruit- and vegetable-eating species. However, vitamins should always be used with moderation; overdoses will do more harm than good, and forced growth, which is relatively easily achieved with reptiles, must at all costs be avoided.

Reptile food

In the wild all reptiles will either catch living animals or eat living vegetation — obviously the key to a satisfactory diet is freshness. A carnivorous or insectivorous reptile will either see its prey moving, taste-smell it via Jacobson's organ, or feel the heat given off by its body. A vegetarian will detect its food according to its colour or fragrance. Invariably, dry or long-dead food will be found unrecognisable. This can be overcome by giving freshly-killed food to carnivorous species and freshly-picked food to vegetarians.

Drasophila, or fruit flies, are ideal for small lizards, geckos, agamas, and lacertids up to two inches long. In warm weather these flies will gather around over-ripe fruit placed in a vivarium, and can be caught in a glass container and farmed. They have a short lifespan but are prodigious breeders; once established a colony can be maintained indefinitely. Drasophila can also be purchased from biological suppliers who sell them to schools and laboratories for experiments into genetics. If a supply is necessary for a short period some may be purchased from these suppliers: if required permanently, several batches may be obtained with the equipment for extensive breeding, and one's supply reared.

Mealworms and maggots, or gentles are the larvae of mealy beetle and horse-fly respectively. Both larvae and adults are acceptable to lizards, small terrapins, and some of the very small snakes. Mealworms are larger than maggots and have legs at the front and display more tenacity. Both can be bought as bait from fishing stores, although petshops sometimes do have mealworms. Cold will slow down the metabolic rate of either larvae, and they can be kept in a cool place for several weeks. If in clean bran they will fatten and become more nourishing, but one should beware of the sawdust used in some bait shops. This will toughen the skin to keep them on the hook, but will make them unpalatable to reptiles, who will excrete them without digesting them — tough maggots may even start to eat their way out.

Forced-feeding can be used when the snake refuses to eat of its own will. Various foodstuffs may be pulped down for use in the feeding guns shown. With the paper-cone type the food pulp is forced out by rolling up the cone. The all-plastic caulking gun has an adjustable stop which is used for feeding venomous snakes. When feeding non-venomous snakes, the tube may be held in place with the fingers.

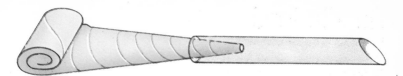

Paper cone and tube

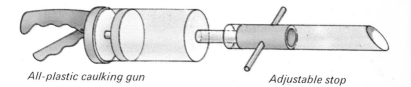

All-plastic caulking gun

Adjustable stop

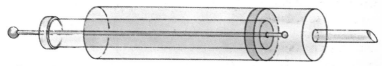

Dual-plunger gun

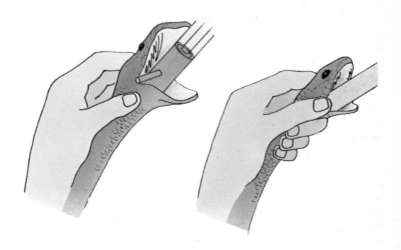

Mealworms and maggots may be bred very easily, but except when small mealworms are required there is little to be gained from this unless they are needed on a large scale. When offering them as food, mealworms and maggots should be cleaned by placing a handful in a kitchen-type sieve and shaking gently. When the bran particles have fallen through, the larvae can be placed in a small feeding dish and presented to the reptiles. This dish should have sides which are unclimbable to the larvae but not insurmountable to the reptiles, which must be capable of seeing the food wriggling around. The authors have watched some lizards spy a food dish from a vantage point on a rock, and on going down to eat find the wall of a dish and no sign of food. Giving up the prospect of feeding, they have returned to their rock, only to see the food again — a perplexing situation. This can be avoided if the dish is sunk into the floor of the vivarium.

If the adult insect is to be offered as food, the reptile keeper must wait and collect the pupae at the stage between larvae and adult

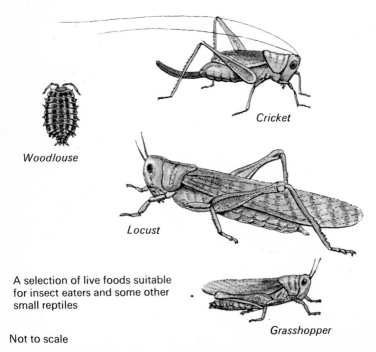

Cricket

Woodlouse

Locust

A selection of live foods suitable for insect eaters and some other small reptiles

Not to scale

Grasshopper

when the body is covered in a hard skin. These can be placed in a deep dish of sawdust inside the vivarium; the increase in temperature will accelerate the metamorphosis, and in a few hours the flies or beetles will be making themselves available to the reptile.

Maggots and mealworms, flies and beetles, may be a staple diet for insect eaters, but variation is necessary especially to include the softer-skinned insects. Woodlice are ideal but they must be caught by the collector himself, not being generally on sale. Crickets, grasshoppers, locusts, and cockroaches will all be welcome, as will small spiders. These also will have to be caught, although cockroaches and locusts can be purchased in bulk. It is most unwise for the novice to embark on breeding these, since both are dangerous pests. Neighbours may not be enthusiastic about even the most innocuous of snakes being allowed out, but the reaction to a plague of cockroaches or locusts would be much more hostile.

Earthworms and slugs have great food value for reptiles. The common earthworm is acceptable to small terrapins and lizards, the

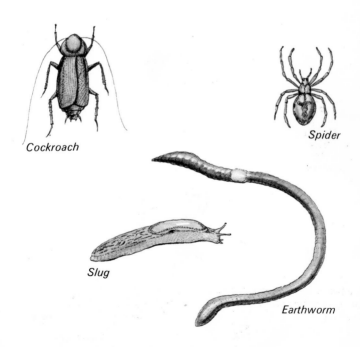

Cockroach

Spider

Slug

Earthworm

Spawn

Tadpoles

Minnow

Frog

Goldfish

Pigeon

Mouse

Chicken

Various animal foods – most of which can be bred in captivity – that can be offered to reptiles. The herpetologist can easily rear frogs and tadpoles from spawn.

Not to scale

small invertebrate-eating snakes such as de Kaye's Snake (*Storeria dekayi*), to the snail-eating snakes (*Dipsadinae*), and to small crocodilians up to one foot four inches or so long. Slugs will be eaten by terrapins, some lizards, and snakes; they can be placed on the greenstuff given to iguanas and tortoises. Similarly, snails complete with their shells are invaluable for the calcium they offer.

Amphibians, fish, and reptiles themselves are all food to certain other reptiles. Frogs and newts are the staple diet of the European Grass Snakes (*Natrix natrix*) and other North American and European colubrid snakes, but it is wrong both morally and ecologically for a herpetologist to catch wild specimens to feed to such species in captivity. It is much better to collect a quantity of spawn and rear tadpoles to adulthood — this can be done without difficulty in a garden pool or aquarium tank, and will provide almost as much interest as keeping the snake. The tadpoles, which may themselves be accepted as food by an aquatic reptile, should first be kept in a plain aquarium in soft water containing oxygenating vegetation such as *Eloden canadiensis* on which they will feed. As they grow, small pieces of meat placed or hung in the tank will provide food. A piece of wood floating on the surface will offer sufficient dry land when the metamorphosis from tadpole to frog or newt occurs. Naturally, the latter will all arrive within a short space of time, so it is as well to kill them painlessly and deep-freeze a supply to be used throughout the year.

Fish are an integral part of the diet of all aquatic reptiles. Small goldfish as sold by wholesale pet traders are usually cheap enough for use as reptile food. Failing this sprats or whitebait can be used, bought either fresh from a fishmonger or deep frozen. Since these are packed and sold for human consumption there need be no qualms about keeping a supply of these seasonally-available fish in the deep-freeze. Minnows and other small fresh-water fish may be worth breeding should a reptile decline to accept goldfish on account of its bright colouring, which might easily spoil the appetite of a poor feeder. Small, cheap tropical fish such as guppies can be tried but since the expense largely outweighs their food-value this will only be a last resort in the case of a stubborn animal. For larger crocodilians and chelonians, large fish such as herrings should be supplied — indeed, salt-water fish should always be included in the diet of any semi-marine reptiles, particularly those crocodiles and terrapins which inhabit tidal waters.

With regard to warm-blooded food, mice, small rats, chicks, pigeons, and chickens are the most commonly offered. What is accepted will depend upon the size of the reptile and its preference for fur or feather; some may eat either. Mice are usually given freshly killed when they are warm and twitching, since this will certainly prompt a reptile to dispose of the food more swiftly. Constrictors will still attempt to kill an already dead animal, a habit quite normal among all reptiles which kill their prey before eating it — cold-blooded and invertebrate prey is usually eaten alive. All the food-animals mentioned here can be bred in captivity. Wild creatures should not be offered. The increasing use of pesticides and fertilisers may result in the contamination of such food and consequently the death of captive reptiles.

The reptile-keeper should be able easily to judge the size of food-animal required by a specimen. A python six foot long would not accept mice, nor a flying snake a rat. If larger food is required for a python or boa, there is little point in providing anything bigger than a rabbit or hare. Raw meat is not much use except when mixed with other food, or when stuffed inside a dead animal to increase bulk. If a snake-eating reptile is kept, the slough of another snake filled with meat may be found appetising. Alternatively, a strip of lean meat attached to a dead snake may appeal. These methods are in common currency, but rubbing a live snake with a piece of meat in order to scent the latter is rarely considered but sometimes effective. One of the authors has had occasion to resort to fixing dead lizards to strips of meat in an attempt to coax a King Cobra to take roughage; this is a major achievement since the King Cobra had been regarded as one of the most difficult snakes to keep. Much can be done by reasoned thought and perseverance on the part of the herpetologist.

Index

*The reptiles illustrated in this book
are coded as follows:*

GREEN

Docile/Harmless

ORANGE

To be handled with care

Poisonous

RED

Dangerous or Potentially Dangerous

Potentially Lethal